Firefighters
at Work

by Karen Latchana Kenney
illustrated by Brian Caleb Dumm

Content Consultant:
Judith Stepan-Norris, PhD
Professor of Sociology, University of California, Irvine

Meet Your
Community
Workers!

magic
wagon

visit us at www.abdopublishing.com

Published by Magic Wagon, a division of the ABDO Group, 8000 West 78th Street, Edina, Minnesota 55439. Copyright © 2010 by Abdo Consulting Group, Inc. International copyrights reserved in all countries. All rights reserved. No part of this book may be reproduced in any form without written permission from the publisher.

Looking Glass Library™ is a trademark and logo of Magic Wagon.

Printed in the United States.

 Manufactured with paper containing at least 10% post-consumer waste

Text by Karen Latchana Kenney
Illustrations by Brian Caleb Dumm
Edited by Patricia Stockland
Interior layout and design by Emily Love
Cover design by Emily Love

Library of Congress Cataloging-in-Publication Data

Kenney, Karen Latchana.
  Firefighters at work / by Karen L. Kenney ; illustrated by Brian Caleb Dumm.
     p. cm. — (Meet your community workers)
  Includes index.
  ISBN 978-1-60270-648-4
  1. Fire extinction—Vocational guidance—Juvenile literature. 2. Fire fighters—Juvenile literature. I. Dumm, Brian Caleb, ill. II. Title.
  TH9119.K46 2010
  628.9′25—dc22
                    2009002384

Table of Contents

Being a Firefighter

Have you seen a big fire truck rush down a street? It holds firefighters. They might go to a house to put out a fire. They use hoses to spray water on the fire. They make sure the fire does not spread to other houses.

Firefighters help people in emergencies. They give first aid to a person who is hurt in a car crash.

Firefighters also teach fire safety at schools. People learn how to be safe with fire and how to give first aid.

Helping Others

Firefighters rescue people and pets from burning buildings. They search buildings and carry out victims. They help victims breathe, and they give first aid.

9

At Work

You can find firefighters in the city and in the country. They work from a fire station. The station holds fire trucks and the tools firefighters use. Some workdays last 24 hours. A group of firefighters work together during a workday.

Some firefighters are volunteers. Often, fire departments in the country are completely run by volunteers.

A firefighter's clothes are important. They are called bunker gear. This gear protects firefighters from burns. The pants and the coat have special thick layers. Shiny tape is on the clothes. Gloves and boots protect hands and feet. A helmet keeps things off a firefighter's head.

The shiny tape on gear is reflective. It helps firefighters see each other in dark, smoky areas.

Problems on the Job

It is dangerous to work as a firefighter. Firefighters can be hurt by part of a building that falls. They can breathe smoke. This hurts their lungs. Sometimes firefighters die at a fire. They risk their lives to help others.

Tools Firefighters Need

Many tools help firefighters do their work. An air tank is worn on a firefighter's back. It helps a firefighter breathe. A flashlight helps a firefighter see in a fire. A firefighter also carries a rope and a knife.

Other tools are used in buildings. An ax or a chainsaw helps firefighters break through walls and doors. A pike is a long stick with a hook on one end. It tears down the ceiling in a room. Fans are put by the doors of a building. They blow smoke outside.

A tool called the "Jaws of Life" is used at a car crash. It cuts metal to free people stuck in a car.

A fire truck gets firefighters to a fire quickly. It has a loud siren and horn. A tall ladder is on top of the truck. It helps firefighters reach high windows. A hose connects to a hydrant. Water is pushed through the hose from a machine in the truck. Some trucks have water tanks, in case a hydrant is not available.

There are different types of fire trucks, including tanker trucks and rescue engines. Most trucks are all-purpose, meaning they can do lots of jobs.

21

Technology at Work

A fire truck has a machine called a GPS that shows a map to a fire. At a fire, a special camera can help firefighters see heat through walls. It is called a thermal imaging camera. The camera shows the heat of the fire, a person, or a pet.

Special Skills and Training

There are different tests a person has to take to become a firefighter. One test measures strength. A second test asks questions. A doctor checks a person's health. A check is done to see if the person has done a crime. A person who passes these tests can then be trained to be a firefighter.

There are different jobs in a fire station. A trained firefighter might become a dispatcher, a fire marshal, or even a fire chief.

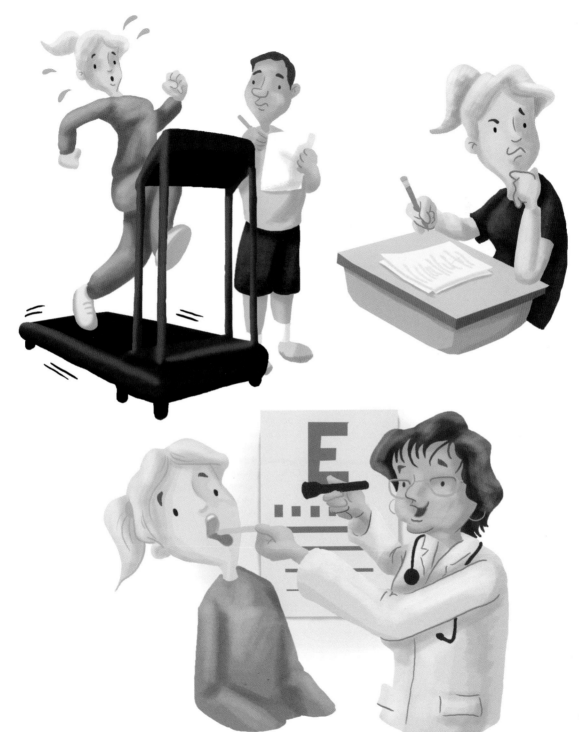

Most firefighters are trained at a special school called a fire academy. A firefighter needs to be calm when there are problems. Firefighters need to be brave and strong. They need good speaking skills. They also need to follow directions well.

Smoke jumpers are one kind of firefighter. They drop from an airplane into a forest or onto a mountain. This type of firefighting requires extra training.

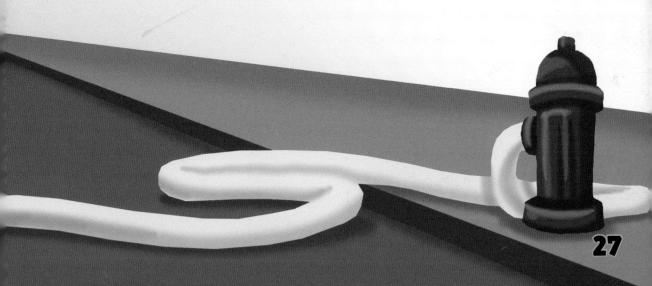

In the Community

Have you seen a building on fire? A firefighter may have helped stop the fire. Firefighters rescue people from fires in homes. They stop fires from spreading from one place to another. Firefighters are important workers in every community.

29

A Day as a Firefighter

Morning

Start work at 8:00 AM at the fire station.
Clean the fire truck.
Exercise to stay strong.

Afternoon

Teach a class on first aid.
Give a tour of the fire station to students.
Make dinner for the firefighters.

Night

Take a nap at the fire station.
Answer a call for a fire.
Get dressed in bunker gear.

Night through Next Morning

Fight the fire.
Rescue two people.
Return to the fire station.
Clean up and leave the fire station at 8:00 AM.

Glossary

first aid—the first care given to sick or hurt people in a crisis.

GPS—Global Positioning System. A machine that helps people find places on Earth.

hose—a rubber pipe that can hold water. Firefighting hoses are covered with fabric.

hydrant—a pipe on a street that goes to water.

layers—pieces of cloth piled on top of each other.

protect—to keep someone or something from being hurt.

reflective—able to shine light back.

rescue—to save someone or something in danger.

victim—someone who is hurt in an accident.

volunteer—a person who gives their own time to work for a cause or an organization.

Did You Know?

🔥 Every 19 seconds, firefighters answer calls about fires.

🔥 Dalmatian dogs have been part of fire departments for a long time. Horses used to pull fire trucks down a street. Dalmatians would run by the horses and protect them from other dogs.

🔥 Sometimes, the color of a firefighter's helmet shows his or her rank, or job, at the station.

On the Web

To learn more about firefighters, visit ABDO Group online at **www.abdopublishing.com**. Web sites about firefighters are featured on our Book Links page. These links are routinely monitored and updated to provide the most current information available.

Index